Edvard Grieg

Peer Gynt

Suites Nos. 1–2
Opp. 46 and 55

Edited by / Herausgegeben von
Richard Clarke

EULENBURG

Contents / Inhalt

EAS 139
ISBN 978-3-7957-6539-2
ISMN M-2002-2363-7

© 2007 Ernst Eulenburg & Co GmbH, Mainz
for Europe excluding the British Isles
Ernst Eulenburg Ltd, London
for all other countries
Edition based on Eulenburg Study Score ETP 1318
CD ℗ 1993 & © 1997 Naxos Rights International Ltd

Ernst Eulenburg Ltd
48 Great Marlborough Street
London W1F 7BB

Preface

Henrik Ibsen's great Norwegian verse dramas, *Brand* (1865) and *Peer Gynt* (1867), stand between the historical plays of his youth and the better-known realist plays of his later years. In some respects *Peer Gynt* is a disillusioned *Pilgrim's Progress*, though Peer shows none of Christian's striving to conquer his vices. He is unashamedly boastful and selfish, a liar and a lecher; yet he is imaginative and fascinating. After raping Ingrid at the end of Act I, he consorts with the legendary Mountain King of Dovre and his grotesque daughters (Act II), sees his long-suffering mother die, and feels a flicker of real love for Solveig. However, it is no great struggle to leave both her and Norway (Act III). Act IV takes place in Africa 20 years later; Peer is a wealthy middle-aged businessman, his money made largely from the Slave Trade. He declines into a Cairo madhouse. Returning to Norway as an old man (Act V) he is shipwrecked, and saves his own life by letting the ship's cook drown. Home at last, he broods for the first time on moral issues, and dies in the arms of the faithful Solveig, who has been waiting for him since they were both young. It is generally recognized that to a large extent *Peer Gynt* is a morality play with universal application, but there is not always agreement as to the precise meaning of its symbolism.

In 1874 Ibsen, revising the play for stage performance, invited Grieg to compose incidental music for it. He even suggested replacing the 'African' act with almost continuous music in which the plot would be mimed and sung; but later he abandoned this idea. In its new form *Peer Gynt* was first performed in Christiania (Oslo) on 24 February 1876, and it was immediately acclaimed. But Grieg was dissatisfied, and 10 years later for a production in Copenhagen, he rescored much of the music, greatly to its advantage. He had written 22 pieces in all, including a prelude, entr'actes, dances, songs and background music. In 1888 he chose four of these pieces for a concert suite, and another four in 1891 for a second suite. The first suite, though not the better of the two, has always been the more popular; together they made the title of Ibsen's play familiar all over Western Europe. Grieg was persuaded to make piano arrangements of the suites, but some of the pieces were so orchestral in conception that they are quite ineffective in this form. The complete *Peer Gynt* score was not published until Grieg was dead; publication made possible the play's huge success in Germany, the Berlin production of 1913 being outstanding.

The eight pieces that form the suites occur in the play in the following order:

Ingrid's Lament. Entr'acte between Acts I and II. Peer has carried Ingrid up into the mountains on the day when she was to have married someone else, and at the start of Act II he abandons her. The heartfelt music gives Ingrid a depth denied her by Ibsen, who showed no interest in the character. The quick theme (bars 1–4) is Peer's *leitmotiv*, established in the Prelude; here, according to Grieg, it represents Peer telling Ingrid to 'go to the devil'.

The Hall of the Mountain King comes at the start of Act II, scene vi, and is grotesque ballet music for the wild daughters of the King of Dovre. They torment and threaten Peer because he has seduced one of them, and in the play they all shout 'Kill him!' on the big chords after letter D.

Solveig's Song comes as an Entr'acte before III.iii, in which Peer and Solveig part affectionately. The main tune, first heard in the Prelude, recurs as a song in IV.x (in Africa Peer has a vision of Solveig in Norway), and Solveig sings it again in V.v, this time unaccompanied.

The Death of Åse (Peer's mother) is first heard as an Entr'acte before III.iv, and then repeated as background music while Peer, unaware that his mother dies as he speaks, sits on her bed and tells her yet another of his outrageous stories. The contrast between the ebullient dialogue and the tragic truth-telling music is wonderfully effective.

Morning, intended as a prelude to IV.v, was played before the first scene of Act IV, where it makes an unsuitable introduction to the farcical dialogue of Peer and his big-business friends. In any case the music suggests a Norwegian dawn rather than one on the coast of Morocco. Grieg wrote of it: 'I imagine the sun breaking through the clouds at the first forte'.

Arabian Dance. The scene is an Arab tent in an oasis, and in the play the music is sung as well as danced by Arab girls. Anitra alone sings and dances the A minor episode.

Anitra's Dance comes later in the same scene, much of it as a background while Peer is speaking; that is why it is so lightly scored. At the end of the scene Peer and Anitra become lovers.

Peer Gynt's Homecoming, played immediately before Act V, depicts the storm at sea off the coast of Norway. According to the composer, the passage after letter C represents the ship sinking; the timpani, bass drum and 'tremolo' basses, he wrote, 'must make a terrific noise [...] All the crescendos and diminuendos must be brought out strongly, and the tempo must be very fluid'. Grieg never wrote for orchestra with more skill than in this piece.

Since the Second World War, it has been generally felt both in Norway and elsewhere that Grieg's score is no longer satisfactory in conjunction with modern productions of Ibsen's play; in any case, few theatres today have the musical resources to attempt it. However, the two suites are very much alive in the concert-hall. Indeed, the music continues to reach a wider public than the play.

Roger Fiske

Vorwort

Henrik Ibsens große norwegische Versdramen *Brand* (1865) und *Peer Gynt* (1867) stehen zwischen seinen historischen Jugendstücken und den bekannteren realistischen Dramen aus den späteren Jahren. In gewissem Sinne ist *Peer Gynt* ein *Pilgrim's Progress* (*Die Pilgerreise aus dieser Welt in die zukünftige*, John Bunyan, 1628-1688) ohne Illusionen, obgleich Peer sich keineswegs nach Christenweise bemüht, seine Laster zu bezwingen. Er prahlt schamlos und ist selbstsüchtig, er ist ein Lügner und ein Lüstling - trotzdem hat er Phantasie und wirkt faszinierend. Nachdem er Ingrid am Ende des ersten Aktes vergewaltigt hat, begibt er sich zu dem legendären Bergkönig, dem Dovrealten, und seinen grotesken Töchtern (im zweiten Akt), wohnt dem Tode seiner duldsamen Mutter bei und fühlt sogar eine Spur echter Liebe für Solveig. Doch kostet es ihn wenig Überwindung, sowohl Solveig als auch Norwegen (im dritten Akt) zu verlassen. Der Schauplatz des vierten Aktes ist Afrika, zwanzig Jahre später. Peer ist nun ein reicher, nicht mehr junger Geschäftsmann, der sein Geld zum größten Teil als Sklavenhändler verdient hat. Sein Niedergang endet in einer Irrenanstalt in Kairo. Im fünften Akt ist er ein alter Mann. Auf seinem Rückweg nach Norwegen wird er schiffbrüchig und rettet sein eigenes Leben, indem er den Schiffskoch ertrinken lässt. Endlich zu Hause, denkt er zum ersten Mal über moralische Fragen nach und stirbt in den Armen seiner treuen Solveig, die auf ihn seit ihrer beider Jugend gewartet hat. Allgemein wird *Peer Gynt* in vieler Hinsicht zu den Moralstücken mit universaler Geltung gezählt, über die spezifische Bedeutung seiner Symbolik ist man sich jedoch nicht immer einig.

Ibsen überarbeitete das Stück 1874 fur die Bühne und bat Grieg, eine Bühnenmusik dazu zu schreiben. Er schlug sogar vor, den „afrikanischen" Akt durch fast pausenlose Musik zu ersetzen, zu der die Handlung gesungen und pantomimisch dargestellt werden sollte. Später gab er diese Idee allerdings wieder auf. *Peer Gynt* wurde zum ersten Mal in der neuen Fassung am 24. Februar 1876 in Christiania (Oslo) aufgeführt und wurde sogleich zu einem großen Erfolg. Da Grieg aber mit seiner Arbeit nicht zufrieden war, schrieb er die Bühnenmusik zehn Jahre später für eine Aufführung in Kopenhagen um, was der Partitur sehr zugute kam. Insgesamt hatte er 22 Stücke geschrieben, darunter ein Vorspiel, Intermezzi, Tänze, Lieder und Musik als Tonkulisse. 1888 schloss er vier dieser Stücke zu einer Konzertsuite zusammen und 1891 wählte er vier weitere Stücke fur eine zweite Suite. Die erste Suite, obgleich nicht die bessere, ist stets die beliebtere gewesen. Beide Suiten haben den Titel von Ibsens Stück in ganz Westeuropa berühmt gemacht. Grieg liess sich dazu bewegen, die Suiten für Klavier zu arrangieren, doch waren einige der Stücke so orchestral konzipiert, dass sie in dieser Fassung ihre Wirkung verloren. Die vollständige *Peer Gynt*-Partitur erschien erst nach Griegs Tod, und ihre Veröffentlichung verhalf dem Stück zu einem ungeheuren Erfolg in Deutschland, zumal bei der hervorragenden Berliner Aufführung von 1913.

Die acht Stücke, aus denen die Suiten bestehen, erscheinen im Schauspiel in der folgenden Reihenfolge:

Der Brautraub (*Ingrids Klage*). Zwischenaktmusik zwischen dem ersten und zweiten Akt. Peer hat Ingrid am Tage ihrer Heirat mit einem anderen Mann hinauf in die Berge getragen. Am Anfang des zweiten Akts verlässt er sie. Die gefühlvolle Musik verleiht der Figur Ingrids eine Tiefe, die Ibsen, der an dieser Rolle wenig interessiert war, ihr nicht gegeben hatte. Das schnelle Thema (T. 1–4) ist Peers Leitmotiv aus dem Vorspiel. Nach Griegs Aussage bedeutet es hier, dass Peer Ingrid sagt, „sie solle sich zum Teufel scheren".

In der Halle des Bergkönigs steht am Anfang der sechsten Szene des zweiten Akts. Es ist eine groteske Ballettmusik für die wilden Töchter des Dovrealten. Sie quälen Peer und drohen ihm, weil er eine von ihnen verführt hat, und im Stück schreien sie alle zusammen zu mächtigen Akkorden „Schlachtet ihn!" (nach Buchstaben D).

Solveigs Lied steht als Zwischenaktmusik vor der dritten Szene des dritten Akts, in der Peer und Solveig voller Rührung von einander Abschied nehmen. Die Hauptmelodie, die zum ersten Mal im Vorspiel gehört wird, erscheint wieder als Lied in der zehnten Szene des vierten Akts (Peer hat in Afrika eine Vision von Solveig in Norwegen), und Solveig singt sie noch einmal unbegleitet in der fünften Szene des fünften Akts.

Ases Tod (Ase ist Peers Mutter). Das Stück ist zunächst eine Zwischenaktmusik vor der vierten Szene des dritten Akts und wird dann als Tonkulisse wiederholt, während Peer, der nicht merkt, dass seine Mutter im Sterben liegt, an ihrem Bett sitzend ihr, wie so oft, eine seiner schändlichen Geschichten erzählt. Der Kontrast zwischen dem überschwenglichen Dialog und der tragischen Musik, die das wahre Geschehen darstellt, ist ungemein effektvoll.

Morgenstimmung, zunächst als Vorspiel zur fünften Szene im vierten Akt gedacht, wird vor der ersten Szene dieses Akts gespielt, wo es als Vorspiel zu dem grotesken Dialog zwischen Peer und seinen Freunden, den Großindustriellen, ungeeignet ist. Überdies erweckt die Musik mehr die Vorstellung einer norwegischen und nicht einer marokkanischen Morgendämmerung. Grieg schrieb selbst darüber: „Ich stelle mir vor, dass die Sonne bei dem ersten Forte durch die Wolken bricht."

Arabischer Tanz. Das Bühnenbild zeigt ein arabisches Zelt in einer Oase. Im Stück tanzen und singen Arabermädchen zu dieser Musik. In der a-Moll Episode tanzt und singt Anitra allein.

Anitras Tanz folgt später in der gleichen Szene, größtenteils während Peer spricht, weshalb das Stück so sparsam instrumentiert ist. Am Ende dieser Szene sind Peer und Anitra als Liebespaar vereint.

Peer Gynts Heimkehr steht unmittelbar vor dem fünften Akt. Das Vorspiel beschreibt den Sturm auf der See vor der norwegischen Küste. Nach der Angabe des Komponisten, bedeutet die Passage nach „C" das Versinken des Schiffs. Pauken, große Trommel und das „tremolo" der Bässe, so schrieb Grieg, „müssen einen gewaltigen Lärm machen. [...] Alle crescendi und

diminuendi müssen stark herausgebracht werden, und das Tempo muss sehr fließend sein".
Nie hat Grieg mit größerem Geschick für Orchester geschrieben als in diesem Stück.

Seit dem 2. Weltkrieg ist man in Norwegen (wie überall) der Meinung, dass Griegs Bühnenmusik sich, mit den heutigen Aufführungen von Ibsens Stück nicht mehr vereinbaren lässt.
Davon abgesehen verfügen heutzutage die wenigsten Sprechbühnen über das nötige Orchester. Beide Suiten erscheinen jedoch durchaus häufig in Konzertprogrammen und die Musik
zu *Peer Gynt* hat weiterhin ein größeres Publikum als das Stück selbst.

Roger Fiske
Deutsche Übersetzung: Stefan de Haan

PEER GYNT · Suite No. 1
I
Morgenstemning – Morning-mood
Morgenstimmung – Le matin

Edvard Grieg
(1843–1907)
Op. 46

Allegretto pastorale (♩. = 60)

© 2007 Ernst Eulenburg Ltd, London
and Ernst Eulenburg & Co GmbH, Mainz

4

D

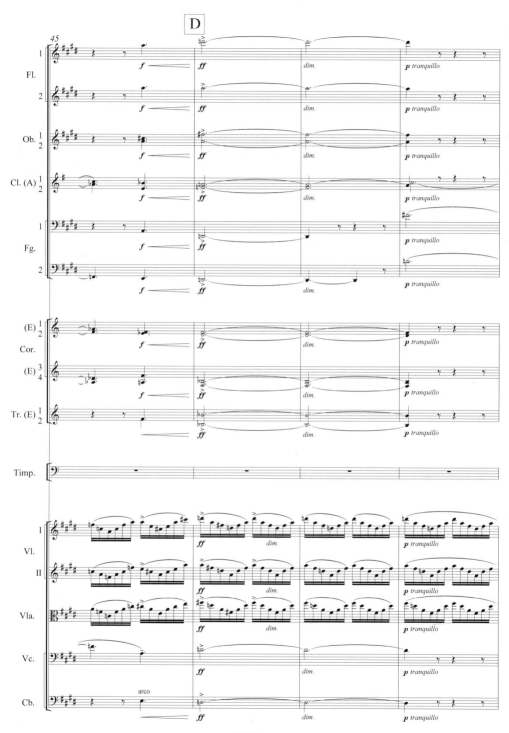

14

II

Åses Død – The Death of Åse
Åses Tod – La mort d'Åse

16

III

Anitras Dans – Anitra's Dance
Anitras Tanz – La danse d'Anitra

poco rit. _ _ _ _ _ a tempo

IV

I Dovregubbens Hall – In the Hall of the Mountain King
In der Halle des Bergkönigs – Dans la halle du roi de montagne

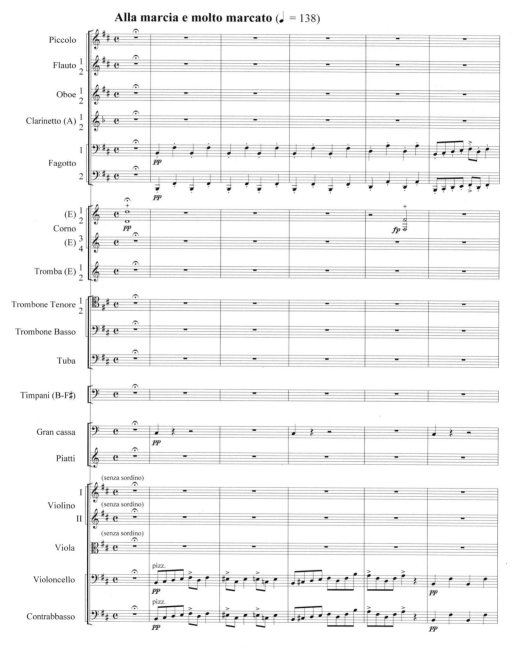

A

57
Picc.
Fl. 1 2
Ob. 1 2
Cl. (A) 1 2
Fg. 1 2
(E) 1 2
Cor.
(E) 3 4
Tr. (E) 1 2
Trbn. T. 1 2
Trbn. B.
Tb.
Timp.
G.c.
Ptti.
Vl. I II
Vla.
Vc.
Cb.
ff
a 2
a 2
8va

36

PEER GYNT · Suite No. 2
I

Bruderovet (Ingrids Klage) – The Abduction of the Bride (Ingrid's Lament)
Der Brautraub (Ingrids Klage) – La plainte d'Ingrid

Edvard Grieg
(1843–1907)
Op. 55

Allegro furioso   **Andante doloroso**

II

Arabisk Dans – Arabian Dance
Arabischer Tanz – Danse Arabe

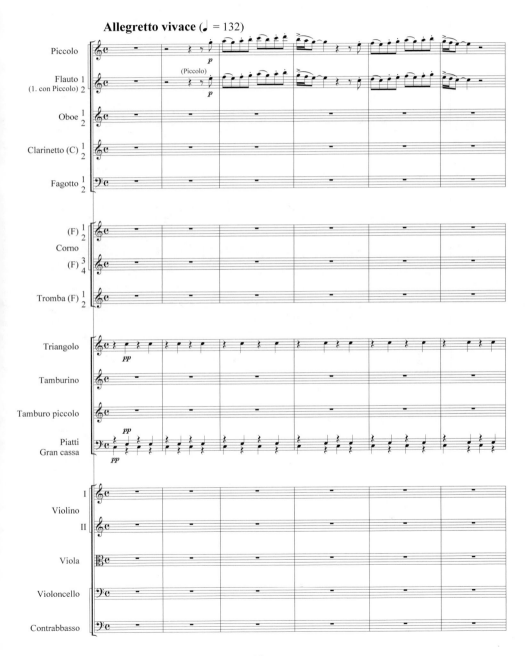

48

poco rit. E a tempo

58

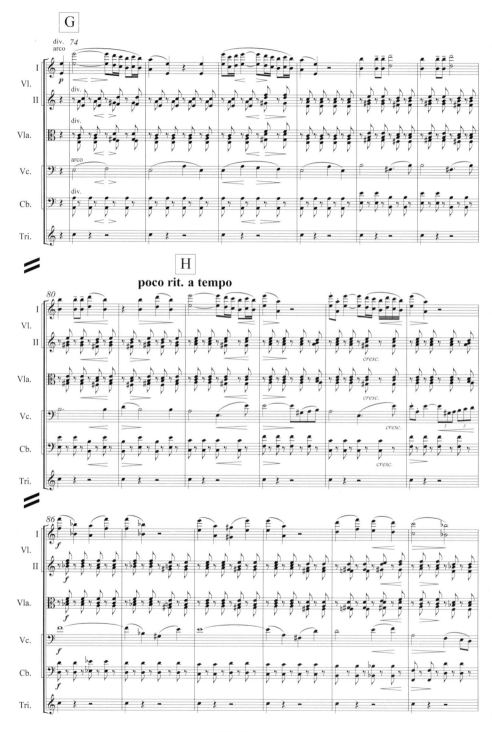

64

68

III

Peer Gynts Hjemfart (Stormfuld aften ved Kysten)
Peer Gynt's Homecoming (Stormy Evening on the Sea)
Peer Gynts Heimkehr (Stürmischer Abend an der Küste)
Repatriement de Peer Gynt (Orage)

EAS 139

E

IV

Solvejgs Sang – Solveig's Song
Solveig's Lied – Chanson de Solveig

poco rit.

Andante (Tempo I)

poco rit.

Andante (Tempo I)